Quintessential
Cubicles

Also by Becky Ventura

Radiant Jukebox: Poems
Wild Rising Press 2021

Quintessential
Cubicles

POEMS

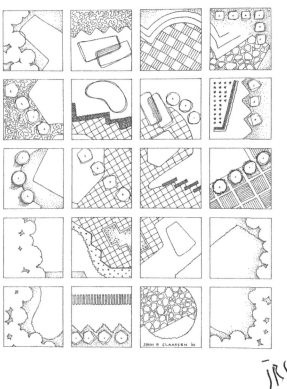

Wild Rising Press

EVERGREEN, COLORADO

Published by WILD RISING PRESS
Copyright ©2024 Becky Ventura.

Editor: Judyth Hill
Book Design: Mary M Meade
Interior artwork by John Regier Claassen

wildrisingpress.com
First edition
ISBN 978-1-957468-38-9

This book is dedicated to my husband, Brian,

and my daughter, Jillian

A WORK OF ART DOES NOT ANSWER QUESTIONS, IT PROVOKES THEM;

AND ITS ESSENTIAL MEANING IS IN THE TENSION BETWEEN THE CONTRADICTORY ANSWERS.

~LEONARD BERNSTEIN, CONDUCTOR & COMPOSER

CONTENTS

ART

LIFE

SPIRIT

ART

Dance in B Minor

Outside, in bitter cold,
our neighbor mightily swings an axe
chopping wood for future fires.

Chopin's Complete Works, Vol. X
lays open on the dining room table,
Mazurka op. 33, no. 4.

Mesto. Pensive, perhaps melancholy.
Melancholy pierces too deeply—
let's agree on pensive.

Softly, hesitantly, music plays.
Broken-winged, she dances.
Sotto voce, a quiet voice interrupts, consoles.

She flutters her wings a bit more,
tired, she rests. Then, a burst of energy ...
inspired chords bounce and leap.

Beautiful dance of give and take, highs and lows,
love and despair, triumph and defeat
repeats its conversation.

Demure, diffident, *dolce.*
Minor turns to major.
Emboldened, she turns coquette,

tosses off her dainty wings,
leaps, pirouettes, until
her inner music box
        winds
            down.

59 Rue de Rivoli

a watery wall
  turquoise
   cobalt
   cerulean

Gershwin's *Rhapsody*
  Debussy's *La Mer*
    Smetana's *Moldau,*
    Ravel's *Jeux d'eau*

crisp snow blankets
  sea breezes
   spring rain
      freshly cleaned clothing

cool stone
 aged beechwood
    metal door pull
    cat's fur

mint tea
 baba ghanoush
honeydew melons
green grapes

trust
  calm
    openness
      reflection

The Age of Wood

She lives by herself inside
a stucco house. This old woman
knows … there's no guarantee
stucco siding won't disintegrate.
She sings a plaintive lullaby,
contemplates houses of wood.

There are many good qualities of wood,
rustic wooden beams inside
her house, a music box (plays Brahms' lullaby)
a wooden train whistle the woman
fears will disintegrate
(though it came with a guarantee).

Warranty? Contract? Guarantee?
Never mind wood.
Like stucco, prone to disintegrate.
Housebound, alone, inside
far too long, the woman
longs for a soothing lullaby.

Lento: tempo for lullaby.
Pretty much a guarantee:
lento is tempo for old woman,
leaning on her elder wood
cane. A voice inside
her suggests: *everything must disintegrate.*

True, all things disintegrate,
even, perhaps, a lullaby.
Go ahead, laugh on the inside,
but an ironclad guarantee

is this: all things decay— wood,
fruit, fish, man, woman.

Just one more thing about woman ...
she doesn't easily disintegrate.
"Here's to Strong Women" asserts a wood
sign. Strong, but gentle, like a lullaby.
No way to guarantee
which emotions are held inside.

What's inside the heart of a woman?
No guarantee, perhaps it'll disintegrate,
Or ... be soothed by lullaby ... knock on wood.

Because of Millicent

Inspired by Adrienne Rich's "For LeRoi Jones"

Dos amigos, playing a duet, cast moon shadows,
an ebony girl, sitting in *ardha vajrasana,* holds a butterfly.

One must dance with eagle's wings—
a Sangre de Cristos warrior never hungers for snow.

From all angles, a mother rocks her child,
four figures gaze heavenward, hands on hearts.

A cottonwood coyote's howl never ends.
In ten steps, a Pueblo woman makes a clay pot.

Eye sockets, yes, but not eyes,
a proper procession includes a banner of Jesus, a rosary,
    and two crosses.

Maestro

Inspired by W. Todd Kaneko's "Dead Wrestlers"

I.

Bradley Cooper puts on his prosthetic nose and changes into Leonard Bernstein.

Lenny. Bradley waves his arms dramatically. Lenny was a much more deliberate conductor.

II.

Bradley Cooper looks longingly at Lady Gaga as she sings. Her mezzo-soprano melody bewitches him. A white fox jumps from Gaga's shoulders. Bradley drops his guitar.

III.

Bradley Cooper slaps a man's bare buttocks and leaps out of bed. He's conducting for Bruno Walter with no rehearsal. He buys a pack of Marlboros and learns to smoke, coffin nails constantly in his mouth.

IV.

We are in the Tanglewood shed. Lenny can barely stand. He leans on the podium railing. Beethoven. Last concert. "Yes, I need to hear that second oboe part," he says. The oboist smiles to himself and plays the passage *forte*. Two weeks later, Lenny dies.

V.

Lenny-Bradley plays piano. No awkward film cuts, no stunt doubles. Segue to Ely Cathedral. Lenny conducts the London Symphony: Mahler's Second.

A euphoric finale.

Mother Holle Triptych

I. HOLLE AND IVY

Inspired by Jane E. Ward's artwork Mother Holle

She sits, in nun's clothing,
book open on her lap,
stirring a cauldron.

Frau Holle, above her,
shakes her duvet,
feathers fly.

Feathers change to snow.
On frozen ground,
blackbirds forage for grain.

Neatly stacked bundles
of wood for her fire,
her warm haven.

Holly and ivy,
a medieval Currier & Ives
Christmas in the village.

Church in the valley,
cottages tucked into pockets,
smoke curls from chimneys.

Well water frozen
covered with snow.
Trees, naked, stark.

White-tailed deer,
hooves raised, greets
morning's first light.

II. *FRAU HOLLE'S APRIL VISIT*

Monday, magnolia blossoms
stood proudly on branches
bathed in sunshine.

Sprays of golden forsythia,
sprigs of grape hyacinth,
crabapple's pink blooms.

Tuesday,
snow falls.
Inside, looking out

at Mother Nature's
cruel little joke.
A mourning dove

tucks her head
under soft
brown feathers.

Perhaps
Frau Holle
is shaking out

feathers again.
After all, we know
it is her job.

III. *WHAT THE ROOSTER SEES*

I spy, with my rooster eye
strewn grain
on sandy ground

hens arguing
clucking
their disapproval

chicks peeping
roly-poly
running 'round

feathers ruffled
pecked
scattered

I take my post
fence post
sentry post

My rooster eye sees
her spiraling fall
down the well

unfolding of
her transformation
from dark to light

she returns
I want to crow
in celebration

she shines
bedecked with gold
I sing her song

From One Vessel to Another

Mirabai says: *I have some light,*
I want to mingle it with yours.

A gray tabby sleeps on a Mexican blanket.
Her breath slow, rhythmic, soundless.
Buddha reclines on a bookshelf
surrounded by Beethoven sonatas,
Chopin waltzes, and Iyengar's *Light on Yoga.*

Kabir says: *Student, tell me what is God?*
He is the breath inside the breath.

We walk. Ducks have left frozen Carpenter Lake.
A doe, on high alert, raises her white tail,
bounds through dead marsh reeds.
She is alone.
Skunk musk lingers in crisp January air.

Near a rock garden
just beyond our path,
a solitary man sweeps cement dust
from a newly molded pavilion.
No need to wait until spring.

Kabir knows the sound
of the ecstatic flute.

Winter's breath.
Breath
of deep
inner
stillness.

Programme

She rests her hand on the piano, takes a breath.
  Anticipation. Music sings.
Shoebox auditorium, Detroit, Michigan. Music rings.

Dancing inside, quiet and still outside. Love.
Oboe, reeds, violin, bow, scores, stand, tuner. Music things.

Mozart dreams of his father, a black mask. Terror.
Lacrimosa dies illa … dona eis requiem … Music stings.

Sublime and ridiculous meet. Annoyance.
Mobile phone, mid-concert. Music pings.

Three curtain calls and two encores. Gratitude.
Basses, cellos, violins, violas in backpacks. Music slings.

Rebekah waits backstage for her husband. Patience.
Walking on Woodward Ave, humming leitmotifs. Music clings.

Pictures

Lily pads float in perfect lines
Longways set, ready for the Virginia Reel

Riptide Warning: Swim parallel to shore
Sandy path, travel-worn with footprints

Shining silver river snake winding through the valley
Dusty yellow wildflowers graze hikers' feet

Turtles sun themselves on logs, herons glide on water
Dip, dip, and swing   dip, dip, and swing

Violet carpet, highlighted by sun streaks, soft mist
Trees stand tall, straight, proud, resolute

Headstones lean as if in a reclining chair
Inscriptions indecipherable. Who once lived?

Magritte Quartet

Inspired by the artwork of René Magritte

I. SCHEHERAZADE

Brass fanfare. Ominous, foreboding.

Veiled beauty, oceanic eyes
pearly countenance,
rose-red lips.

She tells a tale
each night
1001 nights
a never-ending story
that saves her life.

Scheherazade's leitmotif: violin & harp

She arrives onstage.
Head in the clouds,
surrounded by pyramids,
Scheherazade shapes her stories.

A nearby glass of water
moistens her throat
as Scheherazade proceeds
with her fairytale filibuster.

II. COLLECTIVE INVENTION

Beached creature,
human legs,
fish face:
a mermaid mockery.

Her gills useless on land,
she cannot breathe.
Her human legs
equally useless.

We gaze at her, transfixed.
No prince will kiss
the lips of this
impuissant fish-woman.

III. Ready-Made Bouquet

She is Magic that he cannot see.
Black suit and derby hat,
he stands, pondering,
hands in his pockets.
We do not see his face.

He gazes at a tree-grove,
his perch, a balcony.

From darkness,
a maiden emerges.
Her long curls flow,
she wears a lacy flowered dress.
She is barefoot.

Rose petals in her skirts,
a mischievous smile on her face.

IV. VICTORY

Inner life, outer life,
clouds usher us
back and forth.

Divine acuity whispers
of secret dimensions.
We enter, enchanted.

Victorian Family Portrait

inspired by W.H. Auden's "Musée des Beaux Arts"

John, age 10, wears
a double-breasted suitcoat
with a white ruff
so as to not soil his neckline.

Elizabeth, age 8, displays two bows
in her curly brown hair.
She is wearing a long-sleeved plaid dress
with a white lace ruffle.

Robert, age 6, sports a jacket
with three-quarter length sleeves
gold buttons and a wide lapel.

Joseph, age 4, poses in a jacket
identical to Robert's.
It looks too small for him.

His eyes have a worried expression
his lips are turned down,
as if he doesn't really want to be there.

Anna, age 3, is dressed
in a beautiful long white pleated dress
with ruffles at the cuffs.

She has curly blond hair with bangs.
Her eyes are closed.
She is deceased.

They Really Nail Me to the Wall

I didn't know I loved Nâzim Hikmet until
I rode on an evening train with him.

I didn't know I loved Billy Collins until
he let me drop a mouse into my poem.

I didn't know I loved Robert Frost until
we stopped by woods on a snowy evening.

I didn't know I loved Judyth Hill until
she charmed my heart with her dazzling wobble.

I didn't know I loved Sei Shōnagon until
she gave me permission to list hateful things.

I didn't know I loved Kaylin Haught until
God said YES to me.

I didn't know I loved Joy Harjo until
her horses waltzed nightly on the moon.

I didn't know I loved William Butler Yeats until
he showed me the golden apples of the sun.

*Nunca supe que amaba a Federico García Lorca hasta
que dijo:"Es preciso comer fruta verde y helada."*

Sweet Baby

Wood coat of rich chestnut brown … burnt sienna perhaps …
In former days, she sported a dark ebony sheen.

She sits, unplayed, in the corner of our living room,
stripped of her artist's bench, keyboard facing a pink wall.

A shiny black seven-foot Young Chang has upstaged her.
Bach English Suites and Chopin Mazurkas sit on its music rack now.

In her day, she was loved,
her ivory keys played by four generations …

"Rudolph the Red-Nosed Reindeer," "Love is Blue," "The Entertainer,"
Bach Two-Part Inventions, Brahms Rhapsody, Bartok Allegro Barbaro.

This piano wasn't just about music.
Our Premier baby grand was a haven.

In 1936, a disappointed little league baseball player
sought solace underneath the piano after pitching a losing game.

In 1966, a little girl who loved art, music, and books
crawled under her to read *Charlotte's Web*.

It's 2023, time for her to retire … she's going south …
ready to soothe a Kentucky family with her magic.

The Poet's Song

Inspired by Marc Chagall's artwork, The Poet

Heart songs, painted blue
emerald cat's awkward kisses
pencil scratching, paused

Mind turning, flipping perspective
music modulates between anguished chords
and a *legato magenta* melody

He carries both songs inside
poetry is his music

Sometimes words tumble out, *molto vivace*
Sometimes everything stops, *grand pause*

This poet spills his wine
considers the cat
resists an urge to snap his pencil, scratch out lines

He purrs now
into his coffee cup
as images begin to reveal themselves.

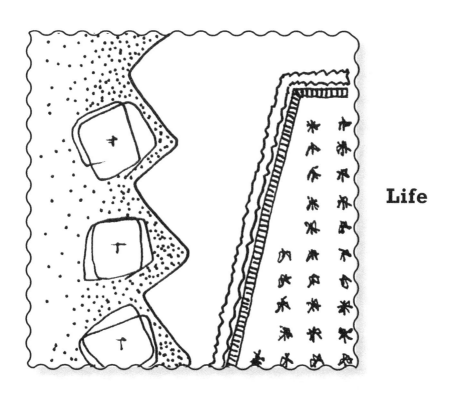

Life

Almas Comes Home

As you start to walk out on the way, the way appears.
  – Jalāl al-Dīn Muhammad Rūmī, translated by Coleman Barks

Chaos reigns in his village.

A little Afghan girl
sells her bedcovers on the street

He seeks to be the humanity
that's missing in his country.

ISIS detonates a bomb
in Kandahar province

He makes a plan.
He will climb mountains.

Jalalabad market burns
Men hang from nooses in public

He carries the clothes on his back
and a dream in his *waskat.*

In Kabul, two boys sob
they cling to their father's coffin

Almas' mother says to us, "Take him, please"
she wishes a better life for her son.

Taliban forbids a female law student
to enter Kabul University

Almas walks.

What the Finder Found

Yellow laundry basket, old and tired
held together with silver duct tape
No more clinging on, dig in, dig in
man's fringed scarf, brown and maroon

Knitting obsession caps
dark blue, light blue, off-white
with flecks of brown and gray
winter's battle helmets

Big black trash bag gulps donations
mittens, gloves, hats, scarves
children's pink & purple earmuffs
a little girl's small pink scarf

We took silver saucers outside
a gift from Uncle Jim
hurtled down our little hill
on Walnut Street

Glazed frozen snow
children bodysurf
in ski coats and snowpants
penguins at play

Grab a tambourine
put on dancing boots
Almas arrives from Afghanistan

A Day in the Life

He lies in bed, patiently.
Nurses check vitals, friends visit.

Sun's shining today
lawn mowers and leaf blowers drone.

She's out of eggs
runs next door to borrow one.

A pianist plays Bach's *English Suite*
music drifts out the window.

He sleeps now.
He refuses food and water today.

A woman in pajamas walks to the mailbox
scoops up *The Detroit News,* glances at headlines.

A black and white cat stares out the window
meows at chipmunks and sparrows.

He says he is blessed and grateful. He smiles.
He stays in bed, not moving anymore.

In the bookstore, people look at history, poetry, classics
some sit in chairs to read.

He had a bookstore once. There are books everywhere.
His nieces have boxed them all up.

A Rooftop in Taos

After getting my fingers into Chopin, Prokofiev, and Bach
(Old upright piano, un-tuned, but what does it matter?),
I meander up to the rooftop.

A deck, fairly new, cedar scent still lingers …
a fireplace, burnt logs, soft gray ashes,
fire has licked the adobe stone, leaving two black tongue strokes.

A candleholder with a sun face, rays cut out,
claims its place on the hearth,
firelight flickers through these spaces.

Two large wooden-legged couches
with ample floral and striped pillows
frame the fireplace.

I still hear the Invention in A minor.
Breeze shakes the aspen leaves,
a sound that stirs souls.

A frog Buddha sits patiently on a table
hands folded in his lap,
wearing robes and a Mona Lisa smile.

Taos Ghazal

Eyes slit shut, he has been harmed
He bears witness, he bears weight
Door with gateway on the bottom

Russian woman, stomping grapes behind a monkey's back
She rests in peace here by daisies and Queen Anne's lace
No arms, no legs ... Camelia has an ample granite bottom

Kachina points two arrows at his head
This pen writes mantras, prayers, poetry
Cinnamon settles to the coffee cup's bottom

See sun on Taos mountain from Andrew's balcony
Mabel placed six ceramic chickens outside Tony's room
Morada Lane, a roller coaster ride top to bottom

The Buddha absolves passersby
Those posts look like oversized licorice sticks
"1922" is painted on Mabel's door at the bottom

Hotura Koi

"Hotura Koi" (Ho! Firefly!) is a Japanese children's song.

Ho! Firefly!
In a Nebraska field, tiny lights flash.

Summer. A hint of skunk, steaks on a grill, lilac's perfume.
Fresh-cut grass, lily-of the-valley, musky garden dirt.

Children with jars, holes poked in the lids, search for fireflies.
Later in the night, lids twisted off, tiny prisoners set free.

Glow-worm, candle fly, peeny-wallie, lightning bug.
Moon bug, golden sparkler, firedevil, blinkie.

Luciérnaga, ipurtargi, kelip-kelip, api-api.
Things that we love have many names.

Japanese say: stars that left the skies to wander Earth awhile,
small torchbearers carry souls of the dead, ghosts of warriors.

Aztecs say: sparks of knowledge in a world of ignorance,
glimmers of hope, lights of guidance, beacons of beauty.

Ho, ho, come, fireflies!
Ho! Ho! Ho! Firefly!

Tsukihana

Midori carried the moonflower from Japan
she's always had a green thumb

It bloomed only at midnight—once a year
it started budding, and she knew …

Call your friends, Midori
pour champagne, clink glasses

Lunar-white petals reveal themselves
like a time-lapse video

Help yourself to edamame and hors d'œuvres
drop into *ardha chandrāsana*

Yellow stamens, circular layers
of delicate pearl-white petals

This flower waited in its protective cage
until performance day

We carried it there, pot heavy with dirt
balanced precariously in a wheelbarrow

Moonflower, safe from marauding deer
protected by its wire holding cell

Celebrated, venerated for blooming
while Beethoven's op. 27 wafts from Midori's spinet

On the Rocks

On the lake, swims a swan
in the distance, wails a siren.
She bends her neck in a crescent
shape, catches a fish in her mouth.
Saint-Saëns thought of her as poetry
cello and piano in prayer.

Often we come to prayer
bowing heads like a swan
mumble our sweet, quiet poetry
or implore with loud voices. Siren
-like wails erupt from our mouths
our bodies forming a crescent.

Shape dough into crescent
rolls, loaves, manna, prayer.
Sacred taste in our mouth.
Poison, though, to a swan.
Shriek of a screaming siren
pierces our peaceful poetry.

A tree has been compared to poetry
branches drooping, crescent
boughs, alluring as any siren.
Each leaf, a prayer.
Graceful as a swan
words tumble from one mouth

then another mouth
adds to the poetry
exalts the swan
exalts white crescent

moon in reverent prayer
irresistible as mythical siren.

Preferring the muse to a siren
moving lips, whispering mouth
chants a fervent prayer.
Devotions, sweet poetry
under the crescent
glow, in wake of white swan.

Gentle as a swan, jarring as a siren
soft shining crescent, many a mouth
sings such poetry, whispers such prayer.

Dear Patty

It's been a long time since I've written to you.
It seems that email or text is easier, faster.
We go for quick fixes these days
move on to the next thing
push through mundane chores,
not even whistling.

It used to be my joy to receive a letter,
it is a rare occasion anymore.
Some letters are decorated
with sweet little doodles.
Some are filled
with facts and stats.

Feelings, once expressed in letters,
simply lie dormant.
Emojis take the place of
"I love you."
It really seems
safer that way.

A spotted fawn walked right by me today,
startled when she saw me.
She ran, peeked out from our swing set, ears alert.
I could have taken a photo,
sent it to you instantly,
instead I'm writing about her in my letter.

Not long after, there was a thrumming
of a hummingbird zipping over to the feeder.
Who can get a photo of that?
or the scurrying of the unseen chipmunk

that caused our little cat, Olive, to jump!
She remained by me, harnessed.

All these things are going in my letter.
No big news.
No one's getting married.
No one's getting divorced.
No one's gotten a promotion.
No one's having a baby.

Song for John

Inspired by Pablo Neruda's "Sonnet 15"

*What we have once enjoyed we can never lose. All that we love deeply
becomes a part of us.*
　　　~Helen Keller

For a long time the earth has known you.
Sixty-four years embodied,
some knew you as a carpenter.
We knew you as an artist.

Sparrows and cicadas now carry your voice.
Weeping willows bear the weight of our loss.
Gentle rainfall mirrors our tears,
sunshine blankets us in warm comfort.

You are a part of our consciousness,
flowers that bloom in our heart's garden,
reflected in the eyes of your wife and daughter.

Freed from this earthly form
as angels sing for you.
You will continue to live with us, on earth.

Call of the Wild

I remember our gray tabby, Julie
named after Bobby Sherman's song

Bobby gave up music and acting
to be an EMT

his poster was tacked up on my wall
along with Donny Osmond and David Cassidy

I remember that night I read *Call of the Wild*
late into the night

a sweatshirt thrown over the desk lamp
so as to not wake my sister

she would have told on me
Then I smelled what I thought was burned cookies

Mom was always burning stuff
but it was my bed

Laddie, our collie, didn't bark
Dad put out the fire with flame-proof curtains

the mattress smoldered the rest of the night
on the patio in the backyard

Beals School carnival was the next day
I went, as if nothing happened the night before …

Room with a View

Inspired by Emily Dickinson's "I Felt a Funeral in my Brain"

I felt a presence in her room,
words scribbled on pink walls.
Adolescent feelings speak
of yearning's inner squalls.

A crooked Beatles poster hangs
behind her old twin bed.
Two guitars sit in their racks,
play music in her head.

A piggy bank, still full of coins,
trophies won before,
incense, tarot, scallop shells,
stickers on the door.

Lava lamps and manikin heads,
golden pumps and more.
Dresses hang with tie-dyed shirts
behind the closet door.

Behind these unhemmed curtains see
snow drifting down outside,
upon the unused slide and swings
as memories abide.

St. Ignace

She drives through the dark
in Michigan's UP, Route 2,
unaware of what lies ahead,
best friend riding shotgun.

Dammit. We hit a brick.
There goes the back rear tire.
It's dark, no cellphone reception.
How do you change a tire?

It's been a million years.
Out comes the manual.
Tire Changing—page 20.
Where's that jack?

Reading the manual in the dark
with a flashlight
draws dozens of midges.
They fly into our hair, our mouths.

Tire's jacked up.
Lug nuts frozen on.
We flag down a car.
"Our baby's not sleeping,

We are soothing him with a ride.
Your tire cannot be fixed.
We'll drive you to a motel."
We hop into the van, luggage in hand.

Next day, the Ford Escape is towed,
new tire put on.
We hop on I-75 South
and head for Mackinac.

Sonnet

Inspired by William Shakespeare's "Sonnet 73"

Grey skies outside reflect grey sky within.
Cold raindrops fall outside and inside too.
Sadness, unprovoked by any sin
evokes deep yearning, comes again anew.

When sun reflects brightly on white snow
despair releases its relentless hold.
Gently freed from former crushing blow,
heart, softer now, with warmth contained in cold.

When nothing moves or moves molasses-slow
no one can know what this poor soul must bear.
E'en when the sun's rays shine on earth below
melee within, although the weather's fair.

Whatever weather should show up each day,
sweetness and sadness are part of the play.

His Name Was Rocky

Like children looking out the window
checking on the status of their snowman
I look out the window for my sweet feral
we grew to love him
he grew to love us.

Now he lies there so still
you'd think he was sleeping,
if it wasn't for the rain.
(Rocky always hides from rain.)
Or perhaps it's a raccoon
and not my Rocky.

But it is my Rocky.

I gaze through the window
and realize what has happened.
A primal cry I didn't know existed
emerges from my throat—
almost can't breathe.

A doe wanders into the backyard,
she sees Rocky and wonders,
Is this quiet little creature still alive?

Tentatively she approaches,
sniffs Rocky gently,
then licks the end of Rocky's tail
and slowly, even reverently,
walks away.

My husband in disbelief on the phone.
His voice breaks.

We share this sadness.

I gently towel off his body,
place our Rocky in a box
lined with an old kitchen towel.

We drive to the vet,
Rocky and I.
They are kind.

Would you like a clay paw print for $35?
Oh yes. I would.
I'll take that baby now, she said.

Chopin's Mazurka in A minor,
playing on the radio, echoes my sorrow.

Rocky knew to come home to die.

States of Being

In Tennessee, violence rains down, fists and clubs.
Cowardly buzzards destroy him, invent excuses.
Our hearts, hurt, crack open. Grief.

In Michigan, the phone rings. It's your mother.
I'm feeling my own mortality, she says.
She is as frightened as she is brave. Courage.

In New York, she plunges 86 stories, finds repose
in a cavernous divot created by her fallen body.
Her gloved hand clutches a string of pearls. Death.

In Nebraska, a lamp sparks, her bed catches fire.
Her sister sleeps, the collie doesn't bark.
Her father rips down a curtain, smothers flames. Gratitude.

In Oregon, he sits, unfazed, in a Japanese-style garden.
On this little bridge, water flows, thoughts float.
He hums, meditates, unaware and aware. *Ananda.*

In Alaska, sun shines on the mountaintops.
Green again, spruce trees welcome warm rays.
Rebirth, recycle, renew, life stirs. Hope.

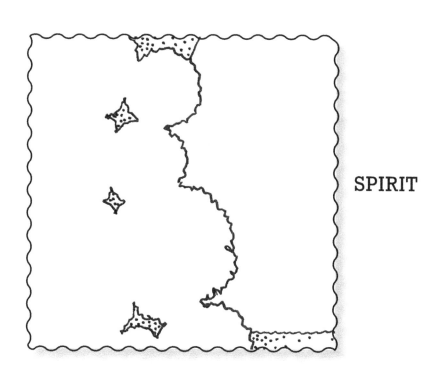

SPIRIT

Life, Divined

A moving web of fascia
in a silver stream
unashamed beings
story within a story

Of a silver stream
antiphonal bird choirs sing
story beneath a story
silhouetted by darkening skies

Antiphonal bird choirs sing
peppered by a dissonant trill
silhouetted by darkening skies
it feels right somehow

Peppered by a dissonant trill
with wings of song, let fly
it feels right somehow
a complicated dance of emotions

Put wings on song, let fly
this condition of unreasonable joy
an exquisite dance of emotions
makes snow fly like feathers

This condition of unreasonable joy
emerges into enchantment
makes snow fly like feathers
the maple tree, still naked

Emerge into enchantment
elixir of honeyed music

the maple tree, still naked
source place of artistry

Elixir of honeyed music
jump into the well
source place of artistry
silence is the frame

Jump into the well
vibrant, multilayered selves
silence is the frame
    [Tacet]

Prayer to the Goddess of Willendorf

Abundant flesh
Red ochre
Fertile, ripe, well-fed

Bringer of babies
Bringer of beginnings
Bringer of beauty

Goddess of Willendorf, hear our prayer

Vulva beneath an ample belly
Strong breasts, like shields
Divine feminine power

Giver of life
Creatrix of humanity
Icon of beauty

The Goddess Makes Herself Known

A bench, mother's lap
an invitation to rest

Two trees cling together
wrapped in an endless embrace

Web womb, filled with pupae
hangs from a branch

Summer sanctuary
a play of dark and light

Trees lean into sunlight
leaves lush from rain

Cavernous canopy
rebirthing those who walk here

Saraswati Reverie

In riverbeds you will find Her
pure, fluid, goddess of speech and music
adorned in white garments with a hint of blue

A royal peacock praises Her
She sits on a lotus flower
rides upon a swan

Flower of Brahman's mind
Her fingers strum her *veena*
Her scarves with tassels spiral down

flutter onto the floor
where She dances
to Her own accompaniment

Om Aim Hreem Sarasvatyai Namaha
She waves to you, as you sit
silently in your earth-shell

Vrksasana

Inspired by Sara & Natalie's Ātma-Sāt-Kāra

Bounteous banyan tree
What is your deepest desire?
Uncoil innate feminine power
Root in luminous vitality

What is your deepest desire?
Prepare earth for future blooms
Root in luminous vitality
Nourishing rich inner life

Prepare earth for future blooms
Fresh green sprouts erupting
Nourish rich inner life
Source-place of sustenance

Fresh green sprouts erupting
Honor the divine Mother
Source-place of sustenance
Remember who we are

Honor the divine Mother
Uncoil innate feminine power
Remember who we are
Bounteous banyan tree

Ode to the Moon

Moon Goddess rises full,
hearts chant her praises.
Ocean tides feel her pull—

lunar magnetism amazes!
The wind may blow
the rain may fall

creatures may take shelter.
Moonlight will glow
upon us all …

we have seen and felt her.

Anansi the Spider knew
Moon's light would not go out.
Young Jack's famous beanstalk grew,

Moon helped his beans to sprout.
In "Buried Moon," a fairy tale,
this globe has come alive

she walks right through the fen.
In the end she doesn't fail
so we can grow and thrive

when Moon's light shines again.

Circular, cyclic Moon,
calendar from times of yore.
Waning, waxing, *clair de lune*

la luna mi amor.
Prayers in moonlight
set intention

'tis a sacred space.
Tranquil night,
no apprehension,

peace has found its place.

Omnipresence

Om saraswatyai cha vidmahe

There is a hum in space
a hum in the galaxy
like a hum of bees
song of bliss
vibrates in your heart
vibrates in your throat
vibrates in your head-crown

Bees know
bliss of buzz
romance of honey and heart
heart chakra
heart nectar
heart healing
omnipresent om

Cat's om is purr
Night's om, crickets and peepers
Interstate om, tires on pavement
Lake Michigan's waves pulse om
Our blood and breath pulse om
Our universe, birthed in om
Om shanti, shanti, shanti

Bhuvaneshwari *Blessings*

May you gaze at the Goddess Bhuvaneshwari
  she sits on a soft petaled cushion
  she holds, for us, infinite space

May your heart open like a lotus flower
  touch divine cosmic spaces
  transmit compassion

May you take your comfortable seat
  sip your tea from a bone china cup
  breathe in ginger & turmeric

May you smile
May you laugh
May you find delight
May you find peace
May you radiate love

May you carry my heart
May I carry yours with me

entombed

our voices quiet for winter
love defies laws of physics
we pull into a shell
face your fears, beloved

love defies laws of physics
a world hiding, concealing
face your fears, beloved
repel insects with blue walls

a world hiding, concealing
connect what seems far apart
repel insects with blue walls
the night we called to the stars

connect what seems far apart
ritual baths, holy water, sea witchery
the night we called to the stars
psychic colors, grapes, passion

ritual baths, holy water, sea witchery
eyes wide open in astonishment
psychic colors, grapes, passion
black pines, streets shine

eyes wide open in astonishment
we pull into a shell
black pines, streets shine
our voices quiet for winter

Kyrie Eleison

Hands washed free.
What is just?
Walk with Grace—
fall to the ground.

What is just?
Thirty pieces of silver
fall to the ground.
Behold your new mother's

thirty pieces of silver,
face on a veil.
Behold your new mother's
timeless path of sorrows,

face on a veil.
Women from town arrive,
timeless path of sorrows.
Do not weep.

Women from town arrive,
escape from this brutal dream.
Do not weep.
They know not what they do.

Escape from this brutal dream.
Love stands faithfully by.
They know not what they do,
learn the way by walking.

Love stands faithfully by
Walk with Grace—
learn the way by walking,
hands washed free.

Golden Girl

In the evenings she set out
to breathe the midnight sky,
bask in moonlight,
bathe in scattered stars.

"Pull us out, before we burn,"
her inner judges railed.
But she stood firm,
that glowing Golden Girl.

T'was to her satisfaction
each dusky violet night
to pull up a silent blanket
of stars, moon, and sky.

"Oh do shake us, wake us up!
Take us with you, Golden Girl.
We'd love to shed our shackles …"
her judges, pleading, cried.

Like the golden rain tree,
with graceful paper lanterns,
and chains of yellow blossoms,
she thrives in tough conditions.

Her inner landscape buoyed
by full moon's radiant light.
Her judges' insistent voices fade,
transmute, into stillness.

What to Put in Your Beauty Cupboard

1 downy woodpecker
1 nuthatch
1 chickadee

Fill your hand with birdseed.
Feed the birds.

1 *National Geographic*
1 Metropark pass
1 pair walking shoes

Wear the shoes. Walk in the woods.
If raining, daydream and look at the magazine.

1 rose quartz
1 carnelian stone
1 amethyst crystal

Get your chakras in order.
Sit still and breathe.

1 medium Saraswati murti
1 sandalwood candle
1 multicolored crystal mala

Wear the mala or hold it.
Light the candle and gaze at the Goddess.

1 score Chopin Mazurkas
1 score Bach Partitas
1 score Schubert Impromptus

Play the music on your grand piano.
Let sound circulate from fingers to heart.

1 journal or laptop
1 smooth pen
Notes from stashed notepads and phone

Write or type.
See what happens next.

Devotion

Myrrh flows, myrrh flows …
Praise to all that is holy!
Church bells, carillon hymns,
gifts for Shakti's *puja.*

Pines frame rocky ranges.
Sun warms shoulders
of distant mountains,
lines of snow glitter on their peaks.

A bowl sits on a cushion pedestal,
filled with oranges and carnations.
Ganesha offers a heart
from his outstretched hands.

Magpies pay reverence with their chatter.

We stomp, we sing, we dance.
We cry, we laugh, we shout.
We move, we play, we live.
We live, we live, we live!

Saraswati knows
Lala knows
Owl Woman knows
We live in service of the Divine.

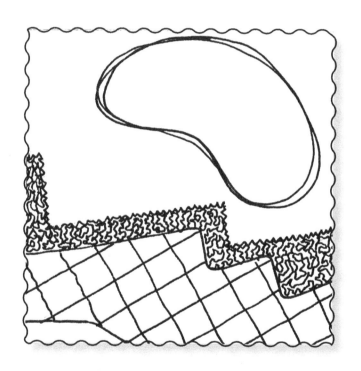

PLAY

Dear Billy Collins...

Inspired by Billy Collins' "Introduction to Poetry"

What would happen if I
dropped a mouse into my poem?

Would she join with others, transform into
a grand white mare, and transport
Cinderella to the ball?

Perhaps she'll skitter
up the grandfather clock in the living room
and stay there 'til the clock strikes one.

She might find her way into a sticky trap
with no way out
or even gnaw a lion out of a net.

Could she be that mouse who ties a bell
around a sleeping cat's neck or
finds her way out of a maze?

She may even become Peanut, a white mouse
with pinkish ears, who served for a time
as a stand-in for a missing hamster.

(She's probably one of the large cartoonish mice
that parades around Disneyland
posing for photos with children.)

But I digress ...

She's sure to be part of a blind trio,
her tail cut off with a carving knife.

Really, though, it's more pleasant to imagine her
frolicking in my piano teacher's attic
with her grandchildren.

Initiation

My first kiss was at a party.
Next-door neighbor's 13th birthday.

His older brother was home,
his parents were not.

We spun a bottle.
It landed on me

and on a boy
whose name I can't remember.

We were sent off
to the closet to kiss.

I asked him if he wanted to—
he said no.

I said me too.
We did not kiss.

The bottle spun again …
We also smoked cigarettes at the party.

Later, my neighbor's mom said,
do you know what happened at Brad's party?

They were smoking!
Oh, I said, looking surprised.

Tell No Lies

Inspired by Pablo Neruda's Book of Questions
(translated by William O'Daly)

Do insects feel pain?
What does the Shadow know?
Who let the dogs out?
Who left their underwear on the floor?
How do you fold a fitted sheet into a
    neat little square?
Why does the caged bird sing?
Are gorillas just very hairy people?
If someone drops a penny off the Empire State
    Building, will it kill a person down below?
Does it take seven years to digest a swallowed
    piece of gum?
How do you mend a broken heart?
What's the point?
How many spiders do you swallow in your sleep?

Ugly Chant

Accident lawyers,
Cabbage Patch Kids.

Calvinism, chauvinism,
colorism, corns.

Culottes, crimped hair,
Deputy Dawg.

Earwigs, bagged mulch,
blacktop, bombs.

Bullets, bullying,
ballpoint pens.

Country Crock containers,
conference swag.

Fast food, fat-shaming,
fondue pots.

Hedge fund managers,
hatch marks on walls.

Junk-food junkies,
Castor-oil spoon.

Icebreakers, sidewalk cracks,
cold, empty rooms.

Waiter, Send This Back!

Fried eggs with runny yolks

Moonie group marriages

High-pitched whine of a dentist's drill

Unreliable internet

Russian oligarchy

Forgotten names or words

Skunks under the back deck

Reminders to sign up for Medicare

Any earworm song (e.g., "Feliz Navidad")

Sorry.

Pick a Little, Talk a Little

Inspired by Miriam Sagan's "Extrimis"

I have won a trophy.
I have worn braces.
I have dreamed I was flying.
I have eaten popcorn for dinner.
I have performed a piano recital.
I have fallen out of a window.
I have stolen money.
I have given birth.
I have a college degree.
I have done a handstand.
I have a small pinky toe.
I have conversed in German.
I have lied, but not in this poem.

Riverwalk

Look! Pee Gee hydrangeas, in Lafayette Greens Garden. Why, Prince Johnson left two Visa cards tucked into a sun sculpture on Joseph Campau Avenue. He would like to buy you coffee at Red Hook, right around the corner. They will make you an oat milk latte with a little heart floating on top. The heart is a wish from your father. Can you see Canada from your hammock? Red Maple Leaf, near Caesar's Casino, waves to the Ren Cen's stars and stripes across the Detroit River. A small airplane flies over the river, toting a Stella Rosa banner, advertising to two different countries.

Is there a poem? Please send it.

Terrence Kennedy, your sunglasses, still in their case, can be picked up at the Aretha Franklin Amphitheater office.

Hey, Lite Brite, how ya doin'?

Regarding Hans

Inspired by "Something About Baltimore" by Diane DeCillis

Our hedgehog, an exotic pet,
was named Quilliam, or Quill,
and not Hans. Hans-my-Hedgehog is

in a Grimms' fairy tale from Germany
although there are also versions of this tale
that come from Lithuania and Czechoslovakia.
Czech Hedgehogs were large

military devices used as barriers to thwart tanks.
They are not small spiny mammals
and certainly not named Hans

although these military Hedgehog devices
were used against German soldiers and some
of them may have been named Hans. My college

boyfriend wished his name was Hans when
he was a child, but he was stuck with the name Joe,
so one day he wrote "Hans" at the top of his school paper

and his teachers humored him. Hans, I mean Joe,
was an excellent pianist but did not play the bagpipes
like Hans-my-Hedgehog. In the Lang *Green Fairy Book*,
the creature is named Jack-my-Hedgehog. I never dated a Jack,

although I understand that Jack is another name for John.
John is the name of my brother-in-law, my brother, my father-in-law
(rest his soul) and my father who is nearly 98 years old
at the time of this writing. My father John,

not Jack or Hans, grew up on farms with hens and roosters.

It is befuddling to think of Hans-my-Hedgehog
riding on a rooster that his father,
whose name might have been John, but

in the German version more likely it was Johann,
saddled and shod for him, but stranger things have happened,
and if you don't believe me just turn on the evening news.

Your skin will prickle, prickle like a chill running through
your body and not a prickle like the name
for a group of hedgehogs.

Mañana

Inspired by Judyth Hill's "Outside in America"

She wears Chanel N° 5 daily.
In yoga class, she was asked to leave.
She loves peppermints and tobacco.

Her clothes are from Salvation Army,
including her wedding dress.
She never married.

She sports a tattoo of
a three-headed dragon
on her left upper arm.

She loves firemen,
drives by the firehouse every day and stares.
The firemen avoid her.

She wants to walk in the park,
but stays inside because her cat
is sitting on her chest and will not leave.

His purr consoles her.

She wears out the left heel of her Birkenstocks.
Her daily routine: lie in bed for 15 or 20 minutes.
Wishes she'd left the curtain open last night.

Go downstairs, feed the cats.
She has a job and if, in the mood,
sometimes works.

Ten Things on a Desk

*Inspired by Wallace Stevens' "13 Ways of Looking at a Blackbird" &
Charles Simic's "Bestiary for the Fingers of My Right Hand"*

I.

101 Joys Make a Rainbow—a small book containing gratitude writings,
such as "I'm grateful for time to learn something new." Usually written in
when the writer does not feel particularly grateful.

II.

A flash drive entitled "20-Hour Yoga Anatomy Training" Scotch taped to
the desk's side shelf. This assures that the item will not become lost in a
desk drawer or accidentally dropped into the wastebasket.

III.

A medium-sized brown and tan-colored Bostitch stapler that contains
five staples. Replacement staples are available when the need arises.

IV.

A yellowed photograph of a young man and woman, both smiling, in a
white heart-shaped frame decorated with tiny pink and red hearts. Both
people have had their hearts broken.

V.

A hummingbird finger puppet, stuck on the end of a pencil, in an old
flowerpot filled with pens, markers, and pencils. It is a ruby-throated
hummingbird, the only kind that visits the eastern United States. I held
one as it died.

VI.

A small box of Puffs tissues, infused with Vicks VapoRub, lying on its side, one tissue protruding. Never buy these unless you don't mind eyes that burn. And certainly do not use in place of toilet paper.

VII.

A hot-pink index card with Christmas gift ideas written down:
MINI LOAF PANS
AMERICAN FLAG
American flag was purchased at Old Glory Flags. Mini loaf pans
    ordered online.

VIII.

A gray and pink Aladdin thermos filled with water and a lemon slice. It was my mother's, a reminder of her practical ways. Her hair was often worn in a neat bun.

IX.

A travel Yahtzee game, in a small wooden cup, containing five wooden dice and a miniature score pad. Unlike most, this cup is quiet when shaken, but the dice, rather rounded, are always falling on the floor.

X.

Stack of Poetry Books by an eclectic group of writers, including:
Alma Almanac by Sarah Winn
Selected Poems of Rainer Maria Rilke, translated by Stephen Mitchell
20 Love Poems and a Song of Despair by Pablo Neruda
Poetry 180 edited by Billy Collins
Presence of Angels by Judyth Hill
The Taste of the Earth by Hedy Habra
The Mouths of Grazing Things by Jennifer Boyden
These books migrate from nightstand to desk to purse, looking for a place to settle.

Fine

Inspired by Diane di Prima's "No Problem Party Poem"

Five speed humps
Fine.
Gluten-free orange cranberry muffins
Fine.
Wine for lunch
Fine.
Rain in the afternoon
Fine.
Open car window
Fine.
Decaf coffee with half-and-half
Fine.
Wrong turn on the way to Bluebird Farm
Fine.
Mabel Dodge Luhan House
Fine.
Barking dog in the distance
Fine.
Cell phone flashlights
Fine.
Glasses off to see better
Fine.
Stacks of papers, some crumpled
Fine.
F'd up, Insecure, Neurotic and Empty
Fine.
I'm fine
Fine.
You fine?
Fine.

Add a coda
Fine.

Mysterious chickens
Fine.
Tamales for breakfast
Fine.
Sixteen words that make music
Fine.
Becky, not Rebekah
Fine!

Slaphappy

Hands: a spoon, fork, and knife.
Pistachios, dates, Quran tonight.

Chameleon's fireball throne,
rainbow's rays, lights on tonight.

There is a death for piano, Federico.
Death mask with black eyes gone tonight.

Silence. Words, form, no form.
Kali, La Mano, Bowler's hats on tonight.

Harmonium Square Dance, Kabir, La Ded,
Remember—wheel, crinkle, Orion tonight.

Deedle, deedle dumpling, my son John, whose
shape and movement verbs yawn tonight.

Lift your hands up, *ay ay ay ay ay!*
Scatter, sizzle, scarlet, beyond tonight.

Acknowledgments

I heartily thank the artists at Wild Rising Press: Judyth Hill, my mentor and Poet Goddess, for her invaluable help in crafting *Quintessential Cubicles,* and Mary Meade for her work designing and producing the final form of this book.

My father, John Regier Claassen, created the front cover and the interior artwork for this book. My great-niece, Norah Catherine Clarkson, created the art for the back cover

I appreciate the Poetry Society of Michigan for providing an artistic forum, and for publishing my poetry in their anthologies.

Poetry Quotes/Credits

"Because of Millicent" was inspired by Adrienne Rich's "For LeRoi Jones"

"Maestro" was inspired by W. Todd Kaneko's "Dead Wrestlers."

"Holle & Ivy" was inspired by Jane E. Ward's artwork, *Mother Holle.*

In "From One Vessel to Another" the line "I have some light, I want to mingle it with yours" is from the poet Mirabai, translated by the poet Robert Bly. "Student, tell me what is god? He is the breath inside the breath" and "Kabir knows the sound of the ecstatic flute" are from the poet Kabir, translated by the poet Robert Bly.

"Magritte Quartet" was inspired by the artwork of René Magritte: *Scheherazade, Collective Invention, Ready-Made Bouquet,* and *Victory.*

The title "They Really Nail Me to the Wall" is a lyric from the song "I Dig Rock & Roll Music" by Peter, Paul & Mary. Several poets inspired this poem:

Nâzim Hikmet: "Things I Didn't Know I Loved"

Billy Collins: "Introduction to Poetry"

Robert Frost: "Stopping by Woods on a Snowy Evening"

Judyth Hill: *Dazzling Wobble*

Sei Shōnagon: "Hateful Things"

Kaylin Haught: "God Says Yes to Me"

Joy Harjo: "She Had Some Horses"

William Butler Yeats: "The Song of Wandering Aengus"

Federico García Lorca: "La Luna Asoma"

"The Poet's Song" was inspired by Marc Chagall's artwork, *The Poet.*

The title "Hotura Koi" is from a Japanese Children's Song.

"Song for John" was inspired by Pablo Neruda's "Sonnet 15."

"Sonnet" was inspired by William Shakespeare's "Sonnet 73."

"Vrksasana" was inspired by the teaching of Natalie Piet and Sara Davidson Flanders, certified Anusara™ yoga and Neelakantha Meditation™ teachers.

In "Bhuvaneshwari Blessings," the line "May you carry my heart, May I carry yours with me" is from "i carry your heart with me" by e.e. cummings.

In "entombed" the line "connect what seems far apart" comes from Judyth Hill's teachings.

"Tell No Lies" was inspired by Pablo Neruda's *Book of Questions* translated by William O'Daly.

"Pick a Little, Talk a Little" was inspired by Miriam Sagan's "Extrimis."

"Regarding Hans" was inspired by "Something About Baltimore" by Diane DeCillis.

"Mañana" was inspired by Judyth Hill's "Outside in America."

"Ten Things on a Desk" was inspired by Wallace Stevens' "13 Ways of Looking at a Blackbird" & Charles Simic's "Bestiary for the Fingers of My Right Hand."

"Fine" was inspired by Diane di Primas's "No Problem Party Poem."

The lines "There is a death for piano" and "ay, ay, ay, ay!" are from Federico Garcia Lorca's poem "Little Viennese Waltz."

"Victorian Family Portrait" was previously published in *Peninsula Poets, Spring Edition*, 2024.

"The Poet's Song" was previously published in *The Art of Listening, December 2023.*

"States of Being" was previously published in *Poetry Pacific, May 2024.*

"Golden Girl" was previously published in *Peninsula Poets, Spring Edition*, 2022.

"Dear Billy Collins …" was previously published in *Peninsula Poets, Spring Edition*, 2023.

Author's Biography

Becky Ventura grew up in Omaha, Nebraska. She was a music education major in college, earning a Bachelor of Music in Education. Her post-graduate work was also in Education, with emphasis on Reading. She studied piano with acclaimed teacher/performer Audun Ravnan at the University of Nebraska-Lincoln. For over 30 years, Becky taught music in the public schools, retiring in 2018 from the Dearborn (Michigan) Public Schools. Over the years, she performed and directed choral concerts, and accompanied and played solo piano in recitals. Becky received the Dearborn Mayor's Arts Educator Award, with US Congressional Recognition, in April 2019.

Becky is a member of the Poetry Society of Michigan. Her poetry has been published on their forum. Becky enjoys reading the poetry of Judyth Hill, Billy Collins, Mary Oliver, Ellen Birkett Morris, Joy Harjo, Robert Frost, and W.B. Yeats.

Becky is also a licensed Anusara™ Yoga Teacher. When attending an Anusara gathering at Estes Park in 2019, Becky had the good fortune of connecting with ebullient poet, Judyth Hill, there. Though Becky had written all her life, she never knew the joys of composing poetry until she met Judyth. Her studies with Judyth continue. Becky has great enthusiasm for the artistry of poetry and music, and it is with a full heart that her poems are written.

Artist Statement

I write from the heart, invoking whatever is living there to present itself, whether it's clear to me or not. I write to evoke remembrance in the reader, whatever that may be. Music influences how I write; my life has been ensconced in classical music, and its forms, phrases and expressions find their way into my poetry, much to my delight.

This collection's body text is set in Adobe Garamond, an Adobe Originals design, and designer Robert Slimbach's digital interpretation of the famous roman types of the sixteenth-century Parisian engraver Claude Garamond and the italic types of Robert Granjon. Since its release in 1989, Adobe Garamond has become a typographic staple worldwide, displaying all the beauty and balance of the original Garamond typefaces.

Claude Garamond was the first to craft letters to the medium of setting type, rather than replicating calligraphy. His letterforms were thinner and more delicate than those before, creating an iconic type that is classy and elegant without feeling overly ornate or showy, a resonant frequency with this poet's relationship to the classic poetry she celebrates and honors in her work.

A marvelously apt choice, the titles are set in Rockwell, a "slab serif" typeface designed by Monotype Corporation's rose-growing engineering manager, Frank Hinman Pierpont, and released in 1934. This sturdy, eminently appealing font, with its characteristically blunt, straight-edge serifs, lends a light note of handmade charm to the text, mirroring the warmth of this poet's personality shining within the poems.

Almost entirely composed of geometrically aligned circles, straight angles, and lines, echoing the collection's title and John Claassen's bespoke and playful artwork, Rockwell feels inviting—just as these poems also combine deep musical and poetic craft and literacy and convey a sense of being invited to tea by a sweet, erudite friend.

Made in the USA
Monee, IL
01 October 2024

66325870R00056